Where Is Baby

Story by Beverley Randell
Illustrations by Ben Spiby

Father Bear went down to the river to fish.

Mother Bear and Baby Bear went, too.

3

"I am going to hide," said Baby Bear. "You can come and look for me."

"Where are you, Baby Bear?"
said Mother Bear.
"Are you hiding
down in the leaves?"

"Where are you, Baby Bear?"
said Mother Bear.
"Are you hiding
down in the grass?"

"Where, oh where

is Baby Bear?"

said Mother Bear.

Mother Bear looked up.

"I can see you, Baby Bear.
You are in the tree,"
said Mother Bear.
"Here I come."

"And here I come,"
said Father Bear.